AF479845

# What's **YOUR** Thinker Thinkin'?

## The Thought Watcher

By Kimberly Blake

Printed in the United States of America

First Printing, 2022

ISBN 9798800657319

Independently Published

To my Beautiful Grandchildren:  Landon, Ava, Gavin, Bella,
Lincoln and Bentley... May your World be filled with
Beauty and Wonder and infinate adventure.

# TABLE OF CONTENTS

# INTRODUCTION

Most of us walk around completely absorbed by our thoughts, so much that we don't even realize we are thinking most of the time. Mindful awareness, becoming aware of our thoughts, gives us insight as to what kind of things we are thinking about most of the day. It gives us the ability to see where we "live", be it a place of constant disruption or harmonious balance.

The purpose of this book is to teach our beautiful children how to become mindfully aware.  This book can be read to kids at a very young age, repeated readings are the best.  My hope is to give this new generation of children a leg up on self-awareness.  The tools are simple and fun, practice makes perfect.  When mindful awareness is introduced at a young age it can become second nature and promote healthy self evaluation naturally.

Do you know *what* your Thinker is?
Do you know *where* your Thinker is?

That's right it's in your head!  It's your brain,
It's where thoughts come from!

What's a thought?
Thoughts are the words that we say to ourselves.
Words we say without talking out-loud.

And thoughts are GREAT!

They can help us to learn new things.
They can help us to solve problems.
And they can help us make our world a beautiful place to live in.

But thoughts can also be very sneaky.
And sometimes not so helpful.
Thoughts can creep up on us without us even knowing it.

So let's try to watch those sneaky thoughts.
Let's learn how to watch what our Thinker's Thinkin'.

Watching can be easy and fun, you just need to know where to look.
Let's start with the things you already watch.
The things that happen Outside you.

# WATCHING THE OUTSIDE

You can watch the things that happen outside you.

You can do this in many different ways.

You can use your eyes to watch the waves crashing on a sandy beach.

You can use your ears to listen to a great song.

That's right!
You can use your ears to watch.

You can even lay back and watch the things that don't seem to move,
Like the stars at night.

And this is fun, you can even watch YOURSELF do stuff... like dance!

**Did you know you can also watch the things that go on inside you?**

There are many amazing things you can watch without using your eyes or ears.

You can do this by just being aware.

Being aware is the same thing as paying attention.

Come on... Let's watch what goes on inside you.

8

# WATCHING THE INSIDE
## Your Breathing

Breathing is something you can watch by just being aware!

Lets try it!

Close your eyes

Big breath in

Big breath out... Ahhh

You got it!

You can watch yourself breathe!

# Your Heartbeat

You can watch your heartbeat by paying attention.

*(Note:  Do you need a little help so you can really feel your heart beat?*

*Stand up and do some jumping jacks and try again)*

# Other Inner Body Feelings

Here's another fun thing you can watch with your awareness!

*(Note:  Don't worry if you can't feel it right away.*

*The more you practice, the easier it gets!)*

# Your Thinking

Here's where it gets really fun.

You can watch your own thoughts!

Try this...

Close your eyes and try NOT to think about anything at all...

It's not easy is it?

What was the first thought that popped into your head?

Isn't that AMAZING?

Thinking happens whether you TRY to think or not!

So now that you know about your thoughts,
you will notice that your thinker is thinking most of the time.
Thoughts come and go like waves.

So what's **Your** Thinker thinkin'?

Is your thinker thinking happy thoughts?

Is your thinker thinking sad thoughts?

Maybe your thinker is thinking silly thoughts?

You might be wondering what the big deal is... so I think a lot, so what?

The thing is, it's important to know **when** your thinker is busy,

Its important to know when you're stuck in your head.

Otherwise, your thinker will just drag you along...

So how **DO** you know when you're stuck in your head?

# CLUES

**You might be stuck in your head if:**

- You've been thinking about the same thing over and over again and can't stop.
- You've been day-dreaming when you should be paying attention.
- You feel irritated, sad, or even angry and don't know why.
- Your brain feels sluggish you can't think a clear thought.
- Or maybe you even have a hard time sleeping at night.

Here are some some fun ways to un-stick those stuck thoughts
and put them in a place that makes them easier for you to see.
We'll call this your **"What's My Thinker Thinkin' Tool Kit"**

# TOOL KIT
## Tool #1
### YOUR BREATH (OR MEDITATION)

This tool will help you to relax.

When you are relaxed, it's easier to see what you're thinking.

**Belly breaths**

*Here's How*

Close your eyes.

Breathe in through your nose slowly, filling your belly with air.

Now breath out slowly through your mouth making an AHHHHHH sound.

(Do this 3 times and sit very still for a few moments)

**Good job!**

# Tool #2



## WATCHING THOUGHT BUBBLES

Notice your next thought.

Imagine that thought surrounded by a clear bubble, like a soap bubble.

The thought might look like words, or even a picture.


What's **your** bubble doing?

Can you see it floating in front of you?

Maybe it's even floating away with all those sneaky thoughts!

Watching thought bubbles is a fun way to notice what your thinker is thinkin'

# Tool #3

## TALKING

Having someone you trust to talk to is very important!

Share your thoughts & feelings with a parent, teacher, or a good friend.

Saying your thoughts out-loud helps you to see what you're thinking.

Believe it or not, sometimes even talking to your favorite
four-legged friend can help!

# Tool #4

## BOX OF THOUGHTS

Have fun and design a box to put on your kitchen counter.
If you have a thought that just won't go away,
write it down and put it in the box.

When you're ready you can take it out and look at it again with your parent or
a friend. You might find that what you were thinking about before
isn't bothering you anymore.

Sometimes things that seem like a big deal now
turn out to be **NO** big deal later on.

# Tool #5





Writing down or even drawing pictures about what you think and feel is another fun way for you to take your thoughts out of your head.  And it's a good way to keep track of what you think about every day.

## *Gratitude, being Thankful!*

Sometimes it is easy to forget about the good stuff in your life when those sneaky thoughts are hanging out and giving you a hard time.  Writing or drawing about the things that make you happy and grateful is a fun way to remind you of all the good things you have in your life already.

*(Note: You can use a notebook or a special journal book for your writing & drawing)*

The more you practice using the tools in your tool kit,
the easier it will be to notice a sneaky thought as it arises.

When you can see a thought as it arises,
it does not have the power to take you away.

So what have you learned?

You've learned that you can watch the things that happen outside you like
 listening to the rain, or watching a baseball game.

You've also learned that you can watch the things that happen on the inside,
like your breathing and your heartbeat.

And then the most amazing thing of all,
you've learned you can actually watch what your Thinker is thinking,

you can watch your own thoughts!

And you can do this by just being aware.

Being aware of your thoughts will help to calm and relax your thinker,

and a relaxed thinker means a happier YOU!

And when you're Happy,

Life is *just* more fun!

## SO WHAT'S Your THINKER THINKIN'?

# THE END

# BOOK DISCUSSION AND PLAY

After reading this book all the way through you can enjoy experimenting on your own while following some of the demonstrations in the book.  You can write or draw or color or paint, you can do it at your house or in your back yard or at the park or in the woods.  With this interactive Book Discussion & Play section you can find out for yourself which tools work best for you, and you can do this in a fun and creative way.

1.  On page 1 the book asks what and where you think your thinker is.  Can you describe what your thinker might look like?  How big is it?

2.  On page 4 we talk about watching the things that happen Outside you.  What kind of things do you see that happen on the Outside?

3.  On page 8 we talk about being "Aware", that being aware is the same things as paying attention.  What kind of things are you aware off right now?

4.  Page 10 talks about being aware of your heartbeat.  Can you describe how that felt? What does your heart look like? Was it beating hard or soft?  Was it beating fast or slow?

5.  Page 11 describes the energy in our bodies as a sparkly feeling.  Were you able to feel that tingly feeling inside your hand or maybe your whole body?  How would you describe that feeling?

6.  Page 13 talks about the "Calm" beneath the waves.  What does "Calm" feel like to you?

7.  Page 14 asks "What's your Thinker Thinkin'?.  Can you describe what you're thinking about right now?

8.  Page 15 talks about being dragged around by your thoughts.  Can you think of a time when you had a thought that you felt was dragging you around?  What was that thought?  How did it feel?

9.  Page 16 talks about Clues.  How do you know when YOU are stuck in YOUR head?  Can you add some clues to this list?

10. Page 17 is a Breathing and Meditation tool.  How did your body feel after you took your "Big Breaths"?  Did you notice your thoughts slow down or maybe even disappear? Describe how you felt in words or pictures.

11. Page 18. Draw or describe your own thought bubbles.  What did you see in your thought bubble? What happened to your thought bubble when you watched it?

12. Page 19. Talking to someone about what you're thinking and feeling. Who is your favorite person to talk to?  Do you have a pet? Can you describe how you feel after you have shared your thoughts with someone?

13. Page 20.  Draw or design and build a box for thoughts.  Do you have a thought right now that you could put into your box?

14. Page 21.  Write down or draw 3 things you are grateful for.

15. Pages 17-21. After playing with all of the "Tools" in your tool box, which tool was your favorite and how did it help you to slow down your thinking? Can you think of a new Tool to add to the tool box?

16. Page 23.  Can you name 3 things that you have learned from this book that has helped you to feel more relaxed and happy?

# GLOSSARY

**MEDITATION:**

Meditation is simply sitting still and quiet, with eyes closed, for a given amount of time; 1 minute, 5 minutes or more if you like.

**AWARENESS:**

Awareness is the act of being able to sense what is happening around you and inside you, this includes sights, sounds, touch, thoughts and feelings.

**JOURNALING:**

Writing your thoughts and feelings or even stories in a notebook or special journal book.

**GRATITUDE:**

Being thankful and happy for what you have in your life right now: Your family, healthy food to eat, good friends, a beautiful park, or even your favorite toy.

**ENERGY:**

When things move they make energy that you can't see.  Even the things that move inside your body like blood and oxygen.

# NOTES

NOTES

# NOTES

# NOTES

# NOTES

# NOTES